FUNDAMENTALS OF THE RESEARCH PAPER

by
William Leahy

KENNETH PUBLISHING COMPANY
BOX 344
PALOS HEIGHTS, ILLINOIS 60463

1983 EDITION

FIRST PRINTING

ISBN 0-913451-05-3

INTRODUCTION

Since students doing library research will encounter various styles of documentation, a decision was made to include three widely used styles of documentation in this edition. These are the traditional footnote style, the popular endnote style, and the newest author-date style. The styles used here follow the styles suggested in two comprehensive style manuals:

The Chicago Manual of Style. 13th ed. Chicago: University of Chicago Press, 1982.

MLA Handbook. New York: Modern Language Association, 1977.

It should be noted that various fields of knowledge (Chemistry, Engineering, Law, Psychology, etc.) have their own preferred style for papers and have their own style manuals. The styles presented in this work are the generally accepted styles used in high schools and colleges. Regarding the newer author-date system of notation, we read from section 15.5 of *The Chicago Manual:* "The University of Chicago Press strongly recommends the author-date system of documentation for all its books in the natural sciences and most of those in the social sciences. Authors in other fields who are willing to adjust their documentation to this system are encouraged to do so." The beauty of the author-date system is that it does away with the needless duplication of the content of footnotes and bibliographic entries. The notes and the bibliography are merged. Also, this system allows for additions or deletions in the final draft of a paper without changing the numbering of notations for the rest of the paper. *Fundamentals of the Research Paper* is designed as a simple inexpensive manual for high school and undergraduate students.

TABLE OF CONTENTS

Page

I. The Footnote Research Paper. 1
   A. General Nature. 1
   B. Title Page. 4
   C. Outline. 4
   D. Footnote Notation. 8
   E. Bibliography. 13
   F. Sample Footnote Research Paper. . . . 18
II. The Endnote Reseach Paper. 26
   A. Endnote Notation. 26
   B. Sample Endnote Research Paper. 27
III. The Author-Date Research Paper. 35
   A. Author-Date Notation. 35
   B. Author-Date Bibliography. 37
   C. Sample Author-Date Research Paper. . 39

THE FOOTNOTE RESEARCH PAPER

GENERAL NATURE

1. Research Paper Defined

The research paper is a documented prose work resulting from an organized analysis of a subject. A documented work is one in which the source of material is credited. The research paper is sometimes called a **library paper** because its preparation involves an extensive use of the library. It is sometimes called a **term paper** because the time allotted is sometimes the greater part of a semester or term.

2. Purpose of Research Paper

The purpose of the research paper is to:

a. enable the student to pursue his own specific interests within a given area of study.

b. enable the instructor to cover general material in group situations while guiding students in specific areas.

c. enable a student to understand the technicalities of a formal paper.

d. enable a student to utilize and combine all skills he has learned.

e. enable a student to gain experience in researching a subject.

3. Parts of a Research Paper

The four essential parts of a research paper are:

a. title page
b. outline
c. essay with notation
d. bibliography

4. Procedure for Research Paper

The following steps are suggested in preparing a research paper:

1. Choose a general subject.
2. Check for books and magazines on the subject.
3. Limit subject.
4. Read extensively and take notes on note cards.
5. Sort note cards.
6. Make trial outline.
7. Read and take more notes on weak areas.
8. Revise outline.
9. Write first draft with notations and bibliography.
10. Revise and rewrite final draft.

5. Notetaking

In preparing a research paper it is desirable to keep notes of information collected on 3″ x 5″ cards. These cards can readily be sorted, arranged, and rearranged before writing the outline or essay. The cards should have (1) a subject heading, (2) the information, and (3) the source of the information. Only one idea and source should be on each card. If time is taken in preparing the note cards, it will not be necessary to go back to the source for the author's name, the page number, etc. All details of the source necessary for notations and the bibliography should be included on the card.

6. Typing the Research Paper

When possible, a research paper should be typed. The text is double spaced and the notes are single spaced with a space between notes. The paper (8½" x 11") should have uniform margins using one side of the paper.

7. Pagination

The sheets of the research paper should be numbered consecutively throughout the paper starting with the first page of the essay. The numbers should appear at the top center **without** parentheses, dashes, quotation marks, a period, or the word **page.** No number should appear on the title page, the outline page, or the first page of the essay; but the next page should be numbered as the second page.

8. Identification

The author's name should appear on the title page under the title in a centered or balanced position. The author's name should not appear on each page or at the end of the paper. Some instructors may want the students to initial each page. The research paper written as a classroom assignment should be kept together with a clip or fastener only at the top left corner in order that both margins will be available for the instructor's comments.

TITLE PAGE

9. Title Page

The front identifying paper is the title page. On the title page is the full title and the writer's name. They should appear in a centered or balanced position. The title of the paper **should not be underlined;** titles are underlined when they are mentioned in the text, in a footnote, or in the bibliography. It is not necessary to indicate that the title page is the title page by labeling it as such. The title page serves as a cover page.

10. Placement of the Title

The title should be repeated three times in a paper. The title should appear on the cover page, at the top of the outline, and at the top of the first page of the essay. The title should **not** be repeated on each page of the paper.

OUTLINE

11. Definition of an Outline

An outline is an organized or systematized arrangement of important elements of a topic. The outline is a patterned summary. The topic is divided into three or four parts. Each of these divisions is then divided into parts. These subdivisions may be divided also.

12. Purpose of an Outline

An outline is used to:

a. prevent wandering off the subject.

b. give a quick over-all view of an essay.

c. insure proportionate space to each part.

d. aid in organizing and giving order to the essay.

e. enable one to spot missing or irrelevant matter.

13. Form of an Outline

The following are guides to the form of an outline:

a. The title of the paper is placed at the top center of the outline. The word **outline** is not necessary.

b. Major divisions are indicated by Roman numerals (I, II, etc.), subdivisions are indicated by English capital letters (A, B, etc.), sub-subdivisions are indicated by Arabic numbers (1, 2, etc.), and further divisions are indicated by small letters, Arabic numerals in parentheses, and then small letters in parentheses.

Title of Paper

I. Major division of topic
    A. Subdivision
        1. Sub-subdivision
            a.
                (1)
                    (a)
                    (b)
                (2)
            b.
        2.
    B.
II.

c. The first section of the outline should parallel the first part of the essay, the second part of the outline should parallel the second part of the essay, etc.

d. The parts of a particular division should be indented equally.

e. A division implies two or more parts. Therefore, logically, an outline should not have a Roman numeral **I** without a Roman numeral **II** or a Capital **A** without a capital **B**.

f. Parallel wording should be used for various divisions of equal rank.

Wrong (Not Parallel)

How to Ride a Horse
I. Mounting a Horse
II. To Start the Horse
III. Control of the Horse
IV. How to Stop a Horse

Right (Parallel)

How to Ride a Horse
I. Mounting a Horse
II. Starting a Horse
III. Controlling a Horse
IV. Stopping a Horse

g. An outline should have its divisions arranged in order of importance, direction, sequence, or interest. Some order that lends itself to a specific subject is to be used.

14. Kinds of Outlines

Outlines can be **Sentence** outlines or **Topic** outlines.

15. Sentence Outline

A sentence outline is one that uses sentences through all divisions. The sentence outline is desired when the material is intended to be used by another person. The meaning is clearer and more exact than a topic outline. End punctuation is used.

American Civil Liberties

I. Freedom from slavery is the foremost right under a democratic government.

II. Freedom of religion is based on the First Amendment allowing its free exercise.

III. Freedom of expression concerns the freedom of speech, press, and other forms of communication.

IV. Freedom of assembly is based on the First Amendment forbidding Congress to restrict people from assembling peaceably.

V. The right to bear arms can be limited by a state's power to have a licensing system.

VI. Equal protection of the laws is based on the Fourteenth Amendment forbidding a state to deny a person equal protection of the law.

16. Topic Outline

A topic outline is one composed of words or phrases throughout all divisions. The topic outline is used for conciseness and brevity. No end punctuation is needed.

American Civil Liberties

I. Freedom from slavery
II. Freedom of religion
III. Freedom of expression
IV. Freedom to assemble
V. Right to bear arms
VI. Equal protection

FOOTNOTE NOTATION

17. Crediting

Crediting or acknowledging the source of material that one uses in a paper can be either **in context** or by **footnote.** Whether the material is quoted directly or paraphrased, the material should be credited. The material is credited to give credit to the source, to enable the reader to verify such things as statistics, to enable the reader to find additional material on a subject, and to give authority to the paper. General information that can be found in various places is not credited.

18. Crediting in Context

Crediting in context is the giving of credit to a source right in the text proper by mentioning it in a sentence. This would save the reader the trouble of looking at the bottom of the page. It might, however, interrupt the trend of thought.

Example of Source in Context

The problem of American behavior abroad is a factor affecting all Americans. Whether tourists or government workers, each American represents America to the other people of the world. In their book The Ugly American, Lederer and Burdick suggest that Americans live with the nationals rather than apart in splendor. They also suggest speaking the language and eating the food of other countries when abroad.

19. Crediting by Footnote

A footnote is a note at the foot or bottom of a page indicating the source of a quoted statement, etc. used in the text on that page. A footnote is sometimes used to define a word or give other information (See page 21). By using footnotes, the date, page, etc. can be indicated with ease.

Example of Source in Footnote

The problem of American behavior abroad is a factor affecting all Americans. Whether tourists or government workers, each American represents America to the people of the world. A recent best selling novel suggested that Americans live among the people, that they speak the language, and that they eat the food of other countries when abroad.[1]

[1] William Lederer and Eugene Burdick, The Ugly American (New York: Norton and Co., 1958), p. 268.

20. Position of Footnote

The footnote appears at the bottom of the page upon which the footnoted material appears. The footnote must be anticipated in order that space will be allowed for the footnote in addition to space for the margin. A small space should be between the body of the essay and the footnote. Some instructors suggest a line be drawn to separate the footnote from the text.

21. Footnote Numbers

A number is placed after the last word of the quoted material to correspond to the number used for the footnote at the bottom of the page. The number is placed before the footnote. Footnotes should be numbered consecutively throughout the paper beginning with number **1**. The numbers after quoted material and before the footnote are slightly above the line of print.

22. Form of Footnote for a Book

The following is the order of the information to be included in a footnote for a book:

a. author's name (first name first)
b. title of book (underlined)
c. edition (only if other than first)
d. city of publication, publisher, and date of publication
e. volume number (only if applicable)
f. page or pages cited in full numbers (with p. or pp. before numbers)

Sample Footnotes
(one author)

[1] Jack Curtis, The Passing Game in Football (New York: Ronald Press Co., 1961), p. 60.

(two authors)

[2] John Bateman and Paul Governali, Football Fundamentals (New York: McGraw-Hill, 1957), pp. 67-68.

(no author)

[3] The Pro Football Handbook (New York: T. Nelson, 1961), p. 9.

(editor)

[4] Don Smith, ed., The Quarterbacks (New York: F. Watts, 1963), p. 34.

23. Footnote for a Magazine Article

The following is the order of the information to be included in a footnote for a magazine article:

a. author's name (first name first)

b. title of article (enclosed in quotation marks)

c. name of magazine (underlined)

d. volume number (in Arabic numerals)

e. date of volume (year)

f. page or pages where cited material appears

Sample Footnotes
(author)

5 D. Jenkins, "Grand Parade of the Bowls," Sports Illustrated, 19 (1963), 31.

(no author)

6 "Quarterback Quest," Newsweek, 60 (1962), 88.

24. Footnote for a Newspaper Article

The following is the order of the information to be included in a footnote for a newspaper article:

a. author (first name first)

b. title of article (in quotation marks)

c. name of newspaper (underlined)

d. place of publication (only if not in title)

e. date in full (January 1, 1981)

f. section and page (Sec. 1, p. 2)

Sample Footnotes
(author)

[7] Moira Hodgson, "The Luxury of Dining in Solitary Splendor," Chicago Tribune, September 4, 1980, Sec. 7, p. 2.

(no author)

[8] "Fat Get Rich—Or Rich Get Fat?" Wall Street Journal, (New York), September 10, 1980, Sec. 2, p. 1.

25. Footnote for an Encyclopedia Article

The following is the order of the information to be included in a footnote involving an encyclopedia:

a. author's name (if article is signed)
b. title of article (in quotation marks)
c. title of encyclopedia (underlined)
d. edition (year)

Sample Footnotes

[9] William Chipman, "Football in the United States," Encyclopedia Americana, 1951 ed.

[10] "Football," Encyclopaedia Britannica, 1961 ed.

26. Initial Reference Footnotes

The initial reference footnote should include all data listed in the preceding four sections.

27. Second and Later Reference Footnotes

When the same source is referred to several times, repeating the entire content of the initial footnote is not necessary. One should use a shortened form for the second or later references to sources already cited. (The use of "ibid.", "op. cit.", and "loc. cit." are now obsolete according to the **M.L.A. Handbook,** 1977.) When the same source is used the second or third time, one simply writes the footnote number, then the author's last name, and then the page number on which the material is found. Below is an example of quoting from the same sources for the second time from different pages.

[1] J. Marks, "Wheeler-dealers: the Skating Revolution Rolls On," Teen, 22 (1978), 46.

[2] Sharon Boorstin, Keep on Rollin': the Complete Guide to Roller-Skating in America (New York: Warner Books, 1978), p. 52.

[3] Boorstin, pp. 86-87.

[4] Marks, p. 47.

If there are two or more works by the same author or two or more authors with the same name, a shortened title of the cited work is used after the author's last name.

[1] B. Bradley, "You Can't Buy Heart; Team Play," Sports Illustrated, 47 (1977), 102.

[2] Bill Bradley, Life on the Run (New York: Quadrangle/The New York Times Book Co., 1976), p. 10.

[3] Bradley, Life, p. 110.

[4] Bradley, "Team Play," p. 48.

BIBLIOGRAPHY

28. Bibliography

A bibliography is a list of books, articles, etc. about a subject or person or by a particular author. The bibliography page appears at the end of a paper or a book.

29. Kinds of Bibliography

The basic kinds of bibliography are the **practical**, the **working**, and the **complete** bibliography.

30. Practical Bibliography

A practical bibliography is a list of works actually used. The works listed will be the same as those used in the footnotes. This bibliography can be labeled **List of Works Used.**

31. Working Bibliography

A working bibliography is a list of all works consulted whether quoted from or not. The working bibliography shows the extent of research that has been done. This bibliography can be labeled **List of Works Consulted.**

32. Complete Bibliography

A complete bibliography is a list of all available material on a subject. The purpose is to indicate additional sources available on the subject and to indicate the extent to which the subject has been covered by writers. This bibliography can be labeled **Subject Bibliography.**

33. Form of Bibliography

Identifying information for each source is arranged with the second and following lines for each entry indented. Each entry is arranged alphabetically by the author's last name. If no author is given, then the first word of the title is used. The specific information included and the arrangement for each type (book, magazine, encyclopedia, newspaper) of entry is given in the following sections. Below is a sample bibliography.

Hair

Cordwell, Miriam. Hair Design and Fashion. New York: Crown, 1962.

Duncan, F. Martin. "Hair." Encyclopaedia Britannica, 1961 ed.

"Hairdos, New Predictions." Mademoiselle, 53 (October, 1961), 90-93.

"Hair-dressing." Encyclopedia Americana, 1951 ed.

Johnston, J. "Wig Fad Raises Price of Human Hair." New York Times, (September 21, 1962), Sec. 1, p. 43.

Kirtland, S. "Revolt Against Fancy Hairdos." Look, 27 (July 30, 1963), 34-39.

Newberry, Louis. Hair Style Design. Los Angeles: Newberry Publishers, 1946.

"Trend Toward Bouffant Hairdos Among Teen-Age Girls." New York Times, (February 24, 1962), Sec. 2, p. 20.

34. Book Bibliographic Entry

The order of the information for a book entry in a bibliography is (1) the author's last name, (2) his first name, (3) the title of the book, (4) the city of publication, (5) the publisher, and (6) the year of publication. The punctuation consists of a comma after the author's last name, a period after his first name and after the title, a colon after the place of publication, a comma after the publisher, and a period after the date.

(author)

Newberry, Louis. Hair Style Design. Los Angeles: Newberry Publishers, 1946.

(no author)

Harper's Bazaar Beauty Book. New York: Appleton-Century-Crofts, 1959.

35. Magazine Bibliographic Entry

The order of the information for a magazine entry in a bibliography is (1) the author's last name, (2) the first name, (3) the title of the article, (4) the name of the magazine, (5) the volume number, (6) the date of publication, and (7) the page numbers of the article.

(no author—monthly magazine)

"Hairdos, New Prediction." Mademoiselle, 53 (October, 1961), 90-93.

(author—weekly magazine)

Kirtland, S. "Revolt Against Fancy Hairdos." Look, 27 (July 30, 1963), 34-39.

36. Encyclopedia Bibliographic Entry

The order of the information for an encyclopedia entry in a bibliography is (1) the author's name, if given (last name first), (2) the title of the article, (3) the name of the encyclopedia, and (4) the edition.

(signed article)

Duncan, F. Martin. "Hair." Encyclopaedia Brittanica, 1961 ed.

(unsigned article)

"Hair-dressing." Encyclopedia Americana, 1951 ed.

37. Newspaper Bibliographic Entry

The order of the information for a newspaper entry in a bibliography is (1) the name of the author (last name first), (2) the title of the article, (3) the name of the newspaper, (4) the date, and (5) the section and page.

(author)

Johnston, J. "Wig Fad Raises Price of Human Hair." New York Times, (September 21, 1962), Sec. 1, p. 43.

(no author)

"Trend Toward Bouffant Hairdos Among Teen-Age Girls." New York Times, (February 24, 1962), Sec. 2, p. 20.

38. Abbreviations

Common abbreviations found in doing research are:

ca., c.	about (circa)
ch., chs.	chapter, chapters
cf.	compare, confer
et al.	and others (**et alii** or **alibi**)
ed.	edited, edition, editor
e.g.	for example (**exempli gratia**)
f., ff.	and the following page, pages
illus.	illustrated
ibid.	in the same place (**ibidem**) (obsolete)
id.	the same (**idem**)
l., ll.	line, lines
i.c.	that is (**id est**)
loc. cit.	in the place cited (**loco citato**) (obsolete)
N.B.	note well (**nota bene**)
n.d.	no date given
no., nos.	number, numbers
op. cit.	in the work cited (**opere citato**) (obsolete)
p., pp.	page, pages
vol., vols.	volume, volumes

39. Sample Footnote Research Paper

College Entrance Requirements:
Past and Present

by
John Murray

Social Studies
5th Period
September 21, 1983

College Entrance Requirements:
Past and Present

I. Introductory Statement

II. Early Requirements

  A. Content of Requirements

  B. Quality of Content

III. Effect of the War on Requirements

  A. During the War

  B. After the War

IV. Today's Requirements

  A. Problem of Space

  B. Educational Associations

  C. College Guides

College Entrance Requirements:

Past and Present

A review of college entrance requirements shows an attempt to be fair to all students and shows an attempt to recognize all fields of knowledge. Along with these democratizing ideas, there was an attempt to unify and control requirements. At times requirements reflected a need to limit or select enrollment and at other times reflected a need to increase or encourage enrollment. As defects or abuses were recognized, changes were made to effectuate the idea of fair and equal opportunity to all students.

The subjects recommended or accepted for the high school curriculum and the subject matter of entrance tests have changed from time to time. In the beginning the American school system was imported from Europe, and Latin was the universal language of scholarship in the Western world. The study of the Latin and Greek classics in the original made up the curriculum. Colleges gradually began "to accept as a lowly supplement to the classical requirement for admission . . . 'vulgar' arithmetic."[1] In the 1860's Latin, Greek, and mathematics made up the curriculum of the "prep" schools. In 1875 Ohio colleges got together and established the minimum requirements for admission to the freshman class. Their statement was one of the first to mention English as a subject. They said the requirements should be "besides the common English branches, two to three years of Latin . . . , two to three years of Greek . . ., and algebra to quadratic equations."[2] After English came history to the curriculum. In 1902 we read, "The scheme of studies which includes . . . Latin, and . . . Greek, together with the amount of mathematics, English, and history . . . may be accepted as the standard curriculum for

---

[1] Arthur Traxler and Agatha Townsend, ed., Improving Transition from School to College (New York: Harper and Brothers, 1953), p. 120.

[2] H.A. Fischer, "Uniform Requirements for Admission," N.E.A. Proceedings, 29 (1890), 706.

preparatory and high schools."[3] A N.E.A. committee in 1895 prepared a tabular statement of entrance requirements to representative colleges.[4] It was a presentation of the content to have been covered in "fitting"[5] schools in terms of books or their equivalent in acceptable subjects which were Latin, Greek, mathematics, history, and in some colleges German and French. Some colleges were not requiring Greek and this was considered a lowering of standards in an attempt to increase enrollment at the cost of scholarship.[6] The acceptance of more and more subjects as legitimate areas of knowledge was not without its opponents. "I wish to enter a protest against the trend of opinion as expressed in this meeting. The truth is that all these men who so vigorously champion the new studies have themselves gained their power from a study of the old subject——the classical languages. There is no knowing the English language without Latin; there can be no familiarity with modern history . . . , without a knowledge of Greece and Rome."[7] A system of free electives was introduced around 1900 by Stanford University.[8] A struggle still continues for importance or recognition of individual subjects.

Along with the problem of content, quality was under study. "The plain fact is that not one-tenth of the schools called high , maintain a course of study which enables the pupil to prepare himself for admission to Harvard College, or to any other college in the State which enforces its requirements for admission as stated in its catalog."[9] "The feeblest way (of admitting

---

[3] F.W. Moore, "The Equalization of Requirements for Admission into Different Courses Leading to the First Collegiate Degree," School Review, 10 (1902), 217.

[4] W.J. Chase and C.H. Thurber, "Preliminary Report of the College Entrance Requirements," School Review, 4 (1896), 341.

[5] Fitting schools were schools that fit or prepared students for college.

[6] Moore, p. 223.

[7] "Round Table on College Entrance Requirements," N.E.A. Proceedings, 36 (1897), 316.

[8] Traxler and Townsend, p. 126.

[9] Charles Eliot, "The Gap Between the Elementary Schools and the Colleges," N.E.A. Proceedings, 29 (1890), 523.

students) is by prescribing . . . a knowledge of certain books or certain well-defined subjects, and then admitting candidates on certificate of any schoolmaster . . ."[10] "The most effective mode . . ., namely, the method of conducting careful examination in all the subjects acceptable for admission."[11] Oral examinations were used first; then written tests were used when the number of applicants rose. By 1900 nearly 500 independent colleges had been established in the United States. As time went on, each developed its own entrance standard with little reference to each other.[12] In 1909 the Carnegie unit was adopted as a way of bringing some order to the chaos. The Carnegie unit, defined by the Carnegie Foundation for Advancement of Teaching, was the credit given for successful completion of a year's study of one subject in a secondary school. Essay entrance examinations and later objective tests were used.

World War II had an impact on entrance requirements. In the 30's many state testing programs were organized that made objective testing services widely available. These objective tests were perfected in the 40's due to the money and manpower devoted to military and governmental programs. In 1942 the Executive Secretary of the College Entrance Examination Board said, "The passing of the June essay-type examination after continuous use for forty-one years marks the end of an era."[13]

After the war the influx of veterans to college made it necessary to process large numbers of students quickly and caused requirements to be revised. It was found necessary to admit students without any high school. Many individual veterans without high school subjects, marks, units, or

---

[10] Eliot, p. 530.

[11] Eliot, pp. 531-532.

[12] Traxler and Townsend, p. 123.

[13] Claude Fuess, The College Board: Its First Fifty Years (New York: Columbia University Press, 1950), pp. 157-158.

recommendations were able to do highly satisfactory work.[14] As a result of the war, aptitude and intelligence tests flourished.

The 1960's saw the "war babies"[15] reaching the college age which resulted in a space problem. "The problem (of determining who should go to school) is particularly acute in the several states which the state supported universities are obliged by law to admit the holder of a diploma from an accredited high school in the state, 'without regard to mental aptitude or other factors.' "[16] The democratic view seems to be that every one should have a right to try college.[17] Since many public higher institutions are unable to use such criteria as rank in class, grade point average, and scholastic aptitude test scores as a basis of selecting applicants, a rigorous selection procedure takes place during the first semester of the freshman year.[18] Five entrance criteria ranked by colleges in order of importance are as follows: (1) transcript of marks, (2) rank in class, (3) principal's recommendation, (4) record of test scores, and (5) personality description.[19]

The development of many preparatory or "fitting" schools, currently called high schools, and the development of many colleges stimulated the formation of various educational associations. The College Entrance Examination Board was in its origins an attempt to bring law and order to the educational anarchy that existed toward the close of the nineteenth century.[20] The idea of "Fitting" has a modern twist in that there are

---

[14] S.A. Nock, "Admission of Non-High-School Graduates," Journal of the American Association of Collegiate Registrars, 21 (1946), 390.

[15] The birth rate went up during World War II. The prosperity following the Depression is given as one reason.

[16] Laird Bell, "Admit and Flunk," Atlantic Monthly, 210 (1962), 54.

[17] Bell, p. 55.

[18] Traxler and Townsend, p. 125.

[19] Traxler and Townsend, p. 4.

[20] Fuess, p. 3.

admission centers now. These centers serve both students and colleges. They try to match or fit a student to a college. The A.C.A.C. (Association of College Admission Counselors) founded the College Admission Center in Evanston, Illinois, in 1958. The C.A.A.C. (College Admissions Assistance Center) was opened in New York in 1959. They are a clearing house for students and colleges.[21] Two organizations which give aptitude tests to college bound students have become an integral part of college entrance requirements. A.C.T. (American College Testing Program) and S.A.T. (Scholastic Aptitude Test) give tests that are required by most colleges.

A college bound student today should consult one of the many college guide books that are published annually. Lovejoy's College Guide in addition to a capsule description of 3,600 colleges gives career, financial, and special program advice. The College Handbook 1982-83 describes over 3000 colleges giving such information as cost, facilities, and requirements. The complexity of college admission and financing is itself a way of screening students. "Today most college applicants apply concurrently to at least six institutions or more."[22] Equally important to most students is financial aid; and it is suggested that students make a variety of applications for scholarships, work programs, federal aid, loans, and grants. "At least four and perhaps five sources of income beyond the help from his family may be used by a student to pay college costs. These are scholarships, term-time jobs, summer employment, loans, and spread-out savings."[23]

---

[21] J. Jefferson, "Getting into College," N.E.A. Journal, 51 (1962), 23.

[22] Clarence Lovejoy, Lovejoy's College Guide 15th ed. (New York: Simon and Schuster, 1981), p. 8.

[23] Clarence Lovejoy, Lovejoy's Career and Vocational School Guide (New York: Simon and Schuster, 1982), p. 3.

BIBLIOGRAPHY

Bell, Laird. "Admit and Flunk." Atlantic Monthly, 210 (October, 1962), 54-65.

Chase, W.J., and C.H. Thurber. "Preliminary Report of the Committee on College Entrance Requirements." School Review, 4 (June, 1896), 341-412.

College Entrance Examination Board. The College Handbook 1982-83. 20th ed. New York: College Entrance Examination Board, 1982.

Eliot, Charles. "The Gap Between the Elementary Schools and the Colleges." N.E.A. Proceedings, 29 (1890), 522-533.

Fischer, H.A. "Uniform Requirements for Admission." N.E.A. Proceedings, 29 (1890), 706-707.

Fuess, Claude. The College Board: Its First Fifty Years. New York: Columbia University Press, 1950.

Jefferson, J. "Getting into College." N.E.A. Journal, 51 (December, 1962), 23.

Lovejoy, Clarence. Lovejoy's College Guide. 15th ed. New York: Simon and Schuster, 1981.

----- Lovejoy's Career and Vocational School Guide. New York: Simon and Schuster, 1982.

Moore, F.W. "The Equalization of the Requirements for Admission into the Different Courses Leading to the First Collegiate Degree." School Review, 10 (December, 1902), 217-223.

Nock, S.A. "Admission of Non-High School Graduates." Journal of the American Association of Collegiate Registrars, 21 (1946), 390-391.

"Round Table on College Entrance Requirements." N.E.A. Proceedings, 36 (1897), 309-316.

Traxler, Arthur, and Agatha Townsend, eds. Improving Transition from School to College. New York: Harper and Brothers, 1953.

40. Endnote Research Paper

The endnote research paper differs from the footnote research paper only in the placement of notes. When the endnote system of notation is used, the notes are placed on one or more pages at the end of the text and prior to the bibliography. The advantage of endnotes is the ease with which they can be listed without regard to whether there will be space at the bottom of the page as in the footnote system. The main disadvantage is that the reader has to flip the pages back and forth to see the source of the notations.

41. Endnote Page

The endnote page heading should be simply **Notes.** The notes are then listed below. The content and form is the same as that for footnotes (See sections 22-27.). A space should be left between entries. One modification widely used is the use of a number with a period on the line instead of a slightly raised number without a period.

Notes

1. Jack Curtis, The Passing Game in Football (New York: Ronald Press Co., 1961), p. 60.

2. John Bateman and Paul Governali, Football Fundamentals (New York: McGraw-Hill, 1957), pp. 67-68.

3. The Pro Football Handbook (New York: T. Nelson, 1961), p. 9.

4. Don Smith, ed., The Quarterbacks (New York: F. Watts, 1963), p. 34.

5. D. Jenkins, "Grand Parade of the Bowls," Sports Illustrated, 19 (1963), 31.

6. "Quarterback Quest," Newsweek, 60 (1962), 88.

42. Sample Endnote Research Paper

College Entrance Requirements:
Past and Present

by
John Murray

Social Studies
5th Period
September 21, 1983

College Entrance Requirements:
Past and Present

I. Introductory Statement

II. Early Requirements

  A. Content of Requirements

  B. Quality of Content

III. Effect of the War on Requirements

  A. During the War

  B. After the War

IV. Today's Requirements

  A. Problem of Space

  B. Educational Associations

  C. College Guides

College Entrance Requirements:
Past and Present

A review of college entrance requirements shows an attempt to be fair to all students and shows an attempt to recognize all fields of knowledge. Along with these democratizing ideas, there was an attempt to unify and control requirements. At times requirements reflected a need to limit or select enrollment and at other times reflected a need to increase or encourage enrollment. As defects or abuses were recognized, changes were made to effectuate the idea of fair and equal opportunity to all students.

The subjects recommended or accepted for the high school curriculum and the subject matter of entrance tests have changed from time to time. In the beginning the American school system was imported from Europe, and Latin was the universal language of scholarship in the Western world. The study of the Latin and Greek classics in the original made up the curriculum. Colleges gradually began "to accept as a lowly supplement to the classical requirement for admission . . . 'vulgar' arithmetic."[1] In the 1860's Latin, Greek, and mathematics made up the curriculum of the "prep" schools. In 1875 Ohio colleges got together and established the minimum requirements for admission to the freshman class. Their statement was one of the first to mention English as a subject. They said the requirements should be "besides the common English branches, two to three years of Latin . . . , two to three years of Greek . . ., and algebra to quadratic equations."[2] After English came history to the curriculum. In 1902 we read, "The scheme of studies which includes . . . Latin, and . . . Greek, together with the amount of mathematics, English, and history . . . may be accepted as the standard curriculum for preparatory and high schools."[3] A N.E.A. committee in 1895 prepared a tabular statement of entrance requirements to representative colleges.[4] It was a presentation of the content to have been covered in "fitting"[5] schools in terms of books or their equivalent in acceptable subjects which were Latin,

Greek, mathematics, history, and in some colleges German and French. Some colleges were not requiring Greek and this was considered a lowering of standards in an attempt to increase enrollment at the cost of scholarship.[6] The acceptance of more and more subjects as legitimate areas of knowledge was not without its opponents. ''I wish to enter a protest against the trend of opinion as expressed in this meeting. The truth is that all these men who so vigorously champion the new studies have themselves gained their power from a study of the old subject——the classical languages. There is no knowing the English language without Latin; there can be no familiarity with modern history . . . , without a knowledge of Greece and Rome.''[7] A system of free electives was introduced around 1900 by Stanford University.[8] A struggle still continues for importance or recognition of individual subjects.

Along with the problem of content, quality was under study. ''The plain fact is that not one-tenth of the schools called high . . . maintain a course of study which enables the pupil to prepare himself for admission to Harvard College, or to any other college in the State which enforces its requirements for admission as stated in its catalog.''[9] ''The feeblest way (of admitting students) is by prescribing . . . a knowledge of certain books or certain well-defined subjects, and then admitting candidates on certificate of any schoolmaster . . .''[10] ''The most effective mode . . ., namely, the method of conducting careful examination in all the subjects acceptable for admission.''[11] Oral examinations were used first; then written tests were used when the number of applicants rose. By 1900 nearly 500 independent colleges had been established in the United States. As time went on, each developed its own entrance standard with little reference to each other.[12] In 1909 the Carnegie unit was adopted as a way of bringing some order to the chaos. The Carnegie unit, defined by the Carnegie Foundation for Advancement of Teaching, was the credit given for successful completion of a year's study of one subject in a secondary school. Essay entrance examinations and later objective tests were used.

World War II had an impact on entrance requirements. In the 30's many state testing programs were organized that made objective testing services widely available. These objective tests were perfected in the 40's due to the money and manpower devoted to military and governmental programs. In 1942 the Executive Secretary of the College Entrance Examination Board said, "The passing of the June essay-type examination after continuous use for forty-one years marks the end of an era."[13]

After the war the influx of veterans to college made it necessary to process large numbers of students quickly and caused requirements to be revised. It was found necessary to admit students without any high school. Many individual veterans without high school subjects, marks, units, or recommendations were able to do highly satisfactory work.[14] As a result of the war, aptitude and intelligence tests flourished

The 1960's saw the "war babies"[15] reaching the college age which resulted in a space problem. "The problem (of determining who should go to school) is particularly acute in the several states which the state supported universities are obliged by law to admit the holder of a diploma from an accredited high school in the state, 'without regard to mental aptitude or other factors.' "[16] The democratic view seems to be that every one should have a right to try college.[17] Since many public higher institutions are unable to use such criteria as rank in class, grade point average, and scholastic aptitude test scores as a basis of selecting applicants, a rigorous selection procedure takes place during the first semester of the freshman year.[18] Five entrance criteria ranked by colleges in order of importance are as follows: (1) transcript of marks, (2) rank in class, (3) principal's recommendation, (4) record of test scores, and (5) personality description.[19]

The development of many preparatory or "fitting" schools, currently called high schools, and the development of many colleges stimulated the formation of various educational associations. The College Entrance Examination Board was in its origins an attempt to bring law and order to the educational anarchy that existed toward the close of the nineteenth century.[20] The idea of "Fitting" has a modern twist in that there are admission centers now. These centers serve both students and colleges. They try to match or fit a student to a college. The A.C.A.C. (Association of College Admission Counselors) founded the College Admission Center in Evanston, Illinois, in 1958. The C.A.A.C. (College Admissions Assistance Center) was opened in New York in 1959. They are a clearing house for students and colleges.[21] Two organizations which give aptitude tests to college bound students have become an integral part of college entrance requirements. A.C.T. (American College Testing Program) and S.A.T. (Scholastic Aptitude Test) give tests that are required by most colleges.

A college bound student today should consult one of the many college guide books that are published annually. Lovejoy's College Guide in addition to a capsule description of 3,600 colleges gives career, financial, and special program advice. The College Handbook 1982-83 describes over 3000 colleges giving such information as cost, facilities, and requirements. The complexity of college admission and financing is itself a way of screening students. "Today most college applicants apply concurrently to at least six institutions or more."[22] Equally important to most students is financial aid; and it is suggested that students make a variety of applications for scholarships, work programs, federal aid, loans, and grants. "At least four and perhaps five sources of income beyond the help from his family may be used by a student to pay college costs. These are scholarships, term-time jobs, summer employment, loans, and spread-out savings."[23]

NOTES

1. Arthur Traxler and Agatha Townsend, eds., Improving Transition from School to College (New York: Harper and Brothers, 1953), p. 120.

2. H.A. Fischer, "Uniform Requirements for Admission," N.E.A. Proceedings, 29 (1890), 706.

3. F.W. Moore, "The Equalization of Requirements for Admission into Different Courses Leading to the First Collegiate Degree," School Review, 10 (1902), 217.

4. W.J. Chase and C.H. Thurber, "Preliminary Report of the College Entrance Requirements," School Review, 4 (1896), 341.

5. Fitting schools were schools that fit or prepared students for college.

6. Moore, p. 223.

7. "Round Table on College Entrance Requirements," N.E.A. Proceedings, 36 (1897), 316.

8. Traxler and Townsend, p. 126.

9. Charles Eliot, "The Gap Between the Elementary Schools and the Colleges," N.E.A. Proceedings, 29 (1890), 523.

10. Eliot, p. 530.

11. Eliot, pp. 531-532.

12. Traxler and Townsend, p. 123.

13. Claude Fuess, The College Board: Its First Fifty Years (New York): Columbia University Press, 1950), pp. 157-158.

14. S.A. Nock, "Admission of Non-High-School Graduates," Journal of the American Association of Collegiate Registrars, 21 (1946), 390.

15. The birth rate went up during World War II. The prosperity following the Depression is given as one reason.

16. Laird Bell, "Admit and Flunk," Atlantic Monthly, 210 (1962), 54.

17. Bell, p. 55.

18. Traxler and Townsend, p. 125.

19. Traxler and Townsend, p. 4.

20. Fuess, p. 3.

21. J. Jefferson, "Getting into College," N.E.A. Journal, 51 (1962), 23.

22. Clarence Lovejoy, Lovejoy's College Guide 15th ed. (New York: Simon and Schuster, 1981), p. 8.

23. Clarence Lovejoy, Lovejoy's Career and Vocational School Guide (New York: Simon and Schuster, 1982), p. 3.

BIBLIOGRAPHY

Bell, Laird. "Admit and Flunk." Atlantic Monthly, 210 (October, 1962), 54-65.

Chase, W.J., and C.H. Thurber. "Preliminary Report of the Committee on College Entrance Requirements." School Review, 4 (June, 1896), 341-412.

College Entrance Examination Board. The College Handbook 1982-83. 20th ed. New York: College Entrance Examination Board, 1982.

Eliot, Charles. "The Gap Between the Elementary Schools and the Colleges." N.E.A. Proceedings, 29 (1890), 522-533.

Fischer, H.A. "Uniform Requirements for Admission." N.E.A. Proceedings, 29 (1890), 706-707.

Fuess, Claude. The College Board: Its First Fifty Years. New York: Columbia University Press, 1950.

Jefferson, J. "Getting into College." N.E.A. Journal, 51 (December, 1962), 23.

Lovejoy, Clarence. Lovejoy's College Guide. 15th ed. New York: Simon and Schuster, 1981.

----- Lovejoy's Career and Vocational School Guide. New York: Simon and Schuster, 1982.

Moore, F.W. "The Equalization of the Requirements for Admission into the Different Courses Leading to the First Collegiate Degree." School Review, 10 (December, 1902), 217-223.

Nock, S.A. "Admission of Non-High School Graduates." Journal of the American Association of Collegiate Registrars, 21 (1946), 390-391.

"Round Table on College Entrance Requirements." N.E.A. Proceedings, 36 (1897), 309-316.

Traxler, Arthur, and Agatha Townsend, eds. Improving Transition from School to College. New York: Harper and Brothers, 1953.

43. Author-Date System of Notation

The author-date system of notation by-passes the use of footnotes or endnotes by referring directly to the bibliography. This simple method of documentation replaces the numbering of notations by using the author's last name, the date (year), and the page number of the material cited. This information is put in parentheses (Charters 1973, 365) and placed where the footnote or endnote number would be placed in the text. When possible, the notation should be placed just before a mark of punctuation.

(Footnote Method)

Kerouac said he was pro-American and could not understand how the radical political movements of the 1960's could have evolved from his work.[15]

(Author-Date Method)

Kerouac said he was pro-American and could not understand how the radical political movements of the 1960's could have evolved from his work (Charters 1973, 365).

To find the title, the publisher, etc. of the work cited, one looks at the bibliography for the author's name. The author-date notation (Charters 1973, 365) refers to page 365 in Ann Charters' book entitled **Kerouac: A Biography** (See the first entry in the author-date bibliography below.). For second and repeated references to the same source, the author-date notation is simply repeated with the appropriate page number changes.

44. Notation for Work by Multiple Authors

For the notation for a work with two authors, use both last names (Gifford and Lee 1978, 15). For the notation for a work by more than two authors, use the name of the first author and then use either "et al." or "and others" (Montgomery et al. 1970, 20).

45. Sample Author-Date Bibliography

Bibliography

Charters, Ann. 1973. Kerouac: A Biography. San Francisco: Straight Arrow Books.

Gifford, Barry, and Lawrence Lee. 1978. Jack's Book: An Oral Biography of Jack Kerouac. New York: St. Martin's Press.

Ginsberg, Allen. 1970. Indian Journals. San Francisco: City Lights Books.

—— 1974. The Visions of the Great Rememberer. Amherst, Massachusetts: Mulch Press.

Kerouac, Jack. 1957. On the Road. New York: Viking Press.

—— 1959a. Doctor Sax. New York: Grove Press.

—— 1959b. Maggie Cassidy. New York: Avon Books.

—— 1959c. Mexico City Blues. New York: Grove Press.

Montgomery, John, Henry Morley, and Alex Fairbrother. 1970. Jack Kerouac: A Memoir in Which is Revealed Secret Lives and West Coast Whispers. Fresno: The Giligia Press.

46. Notation for Author of Several Works

When a research paper involves several works by the same author, the date is the key to which work is cited. From the bibliography above the author-date notation (Ginsberg 1970, 45) refers to page 45 in **Indian Journals** and the notation (Ginsberg 1974, 103) refers to page 103 in **Visions of the Great Rememberer.**

47. Notation for Author of Several Works Published in the Same Year

When a research paper involves several works published in the same year by the same author, a letter of the alphabet is added to the dates in order to distinguish one work from another. The letters (a,b,c, etc.) are added to both the author-date notation and the bibliographic entry. From the bibliography above (Kerouac 1959a, 30) refers to **Doctor Sax,** (Kerouac 1959b, 55) refers to **Maggie Cassidy,** and (Kerouac 1959c, 67) refers to **Mexico City Blues.**

48. Author-Date Bibliography

The basic difference between the author-date bibliographic style and other bibliographic styles is the placing of the date after the author's name rather than after the publisher's name. The author-date bibliography also requires an author's name at the beginning of each entry. If no name for an author or editor is found on a work, then the association, government agency, university, or publisher is used as the author. This may require repeating that name in the entry.

49. Sample Author-Date Bibliographic Entries with Corresponding Author-Date Notations

"B" means bibliographic entry and "A" means author-date notation.

(Book — one author)

B Goulden, Joseph. 1982. Korea, The Untold Story of the War. New York: Times Books.

A (Goulden 1982, 10)

(Book — two authors)

B Riley, John W., Jr. and Wilbur Schramm. 1951. The Reds Take a City. New Brunswick: Rutgers University Press.

A (Riley and Schramm 1951, 20)

(Book - organization as author)

B Veterans of Foreign Wars. 1951. Pictorial History of the Korean War. New York: Veterans' Historical Book Service.

A (Veterans of Foreign Wars 1951, 30)

(Book — government agency as author)

B Department of the Army. 1952. Korea-1950. Washington, D.C.: U.S. Goverment Printing Office.

A (Department of the Army 1952, 40)

(Magazine article)

B Bell, J. 1950. "Brave Men of No Name Ridge." Life 29 (August 28) 34.

A (Bell 1950, 34)

(Magazine article — no author)

B Newsweek, Inc. 1950. "Invasion at Inchon." Newsweek 36 (September 25) 21-25

A (Newsweek, Inc. 1950, 23)

In the above entry the publishing company, Newsweek, as author is not underlined. The name of the magazine, **Newsweek,** is underlined.

(Newspaper article)

B The New York Times Co. 1950. "North Korea Invades South." The New York Times, (June 25) Sec. 1, p. 1.

A (The New York Times Co. 1950, 1)

(Encyclopedia article)

B Britannica, 1973. "Korean War." Encyclopaedia Britannica. 13: 467.

A (Britannica 1973, 467)

50. Sample Author-Date Research Paper

College Entrance Requirements:
Past and Present

by
John Murray

Social Studies
5th Period
September 21, 1983

College Entrance Requirements:
Past and Present

I. Introductory Statement

II. Early Requirements

- A. Content of Requirements
- B. Quality of Content

III. Effect of the War on Requirements

- A. During the War
- B. After the War

IV. Today's Requirements

- A. Problem of Space
- B. Educational Associations
- C. College Guides

College Entrance Requirements:

Past and Present

A review of college entrance requirements shows an attempt to be fair to all students and shows an attempt to recognize all fields of knowledge. Along with these democratizing ideas, there was an attempt to unify and control requirements. At times requirements reflected a need to limit or select enrollment and at other times reflected a need to increase or encourage enrollment. As defects or abuses were recognized, changes were made to effectuate the idea of fair and equal opportunity to all students.

The subjects recommended or accepted for the high school curriculum and the subject matter of entrance tests have changed from time to time. In the beginning the American school system was imported from Europe, and Latin was the universal language of scholarship in the Western world. The study of the Latin and Greek classics in the original made up the curriculum. Colleges gradually began "to accept as a lowly supplement to the classical requirement for admission...'vulgar arithmetic" **(Traxler and Townsend 1953, 120).** In the 1860's Latin, Greek, and mathematics made up the curriculum of the "prep" schools. In 1875 Ohio colleges got together and established the minimum requirements for admission to the freshman class. Their statement was one of the first to mention English as a subject. They said the requirements should be "besides the common English branches, two to three years of Latin..., two to three years of Greek..., and algebra to quadratic equations" **(Fischer 1890, 706).** After English came history to the curriculum. In 1902 we read, "The scheme of studies which includes...Latin, and...Greek, together with the amount of mathematics, English, and history...may be accepted as the standard curriculum for preparatory and high schools" **(Moore 1902, 217).** A N.E.A. committee in 1895 prepared a tabular statement of entrance requirements to representative colleges **(Chase and Thurber 1896, 341).** It was a presentation of the content to have been covered in ''fitting'' schools (Fitting schools were schools that fit students for college.) in terms of books or their equivalent in acceptable subjects which were Latin, Greek, mathematics, history, and in some colleges German and French. Some colleges were not requiring Greek and this was considered a lowering of standards in an attempt to increase enrollment at the cost of scholarship **(Moore 1902, 223).** The acceptance of more and more subjects as legitimate areas of knowledge were not without its opponents. ''I wish to enter a protest against the trend of opinion as expressed in this meeting. The truth is that all these men who so vigorously champion the new studies have themselves gained their power from a study of the old subject—the classical languages. There is no knowing the English language without Latin; there can be no familiarity with modern history..., without a knowledge of Greece and Rome'' **(N.E.A. 1897, 316).** A system of free electives was introduced around 1900 by Stanford University **(Traxler and Townsend 1953, 126).** A struggle still continues for importance or recognition of individual subjects.

Along with the problem of content, quality was under study. ''The plain fact is that not one-tenth of the schools called high...maintain a course of study which enables that pupil to prepare himself for admission to Harvard College, or any other college in the State which enforces its requirements for admission as stated in its catalog'' **(Eliot 1890, 523).** ''The feeblest way (of admitting students) is by prescribing...a knowledge of certain books or certain well-defined subjects, and then admitting candidates on certificate of any schoolmaster'' **(Eliot 1890, 530).** ''The most effective mode..., namely, the method of conducting careful examination in all the subjects acceptable for admission'' **(Eliot 1890, 531-532).** Oral examinations were used first; then written tests were used when the number of applicants rose. By 1900 nearly 500 independent colleges had been established in the United States. As time went on, each developed its own entrance standard with little reference to each other **(Traxler and Townsend 1953, 123).** In 1909 the Carnegie unit was adopted as a way of bringing some order to the chaos. The Carnegie unit, defined by the Carnegie Foundation for Advancement of Teaching, was the credit given for successful completion of a year's study of one subject in a secondary school. Essay entrance examinations and later objective tests were used.

World War II had an impact on entrance requirements. In the 30's many state testing programs were organized that made objective testing services widely available. These objective tests were perfected in the 40's due to the money and manpower devoted to military and government programs. In 1942 the Executive Secretary of the College Entrance Examination Board said, "The passing of the June essay-type examination after continuous use for forty-one years marks the end of an era" **(Fuess 1950, 157-158).**

After the war the influx of veterans to college made it necessary to process large numbers of students quickly and caused requirements to be revised. It was found necessary to admit students without any high school. Many individual veterans without high school subjects, marks, units, or recommendations were able to do highly satisfactory work **(Nock 1946, 390).** As a result of the war, aptitude and intelligence tests flourished.

The 1960's saw the "war babies" (The birth rate went up during World War II. The prosperity following the Depression is given as one reason.) reaching the college age which resulted in a space problem. "The problem (of determining who should go to school) is particularly acute in the several states which the state supported universities are obliged by law to admit the holder of a diploma from an accredited high school in the state, 'without regard to mental aptitude or other factors''' **(Bell 1962, 54).** The democratic view seems to be that every one should have a right to try college **(Bell 1962, 55).** Since many public higher institutions are unable to use such criteria as rank in class, grade point average, and scholastic aptitude test scores as a basis for selecting applicants, a rigorous selection procedure takes place during the first semester of the freshman year **(Traxler and Townsend 1953, 125).** Five entrance criteria ranked by colleges in order of importance are as follows: (1) transcript of marks, (2) rank in class, (3) principal's recommendation, (4) record of test scores, and (5) personality description **(Traxler and Townsend 1953, 4).**

The development of many preparatory or ''fitting'' schools, currently called high schools, and the development of many colleges stimulated the formation of various educational associations. The College Entrance Examination Board was in its origins an attempt to bring law and order to the educational anarchy that existed toward the close of the nineteenth century **(Fuess 1950, 3).** The idea of ''fitting'' has a modern twist in that there are admission centers now. These centers serve both students and colleges. They try to match or fit a student to a college. The A.C.A.C. (Association of College Admission Counselors) founded the College Admission Center in Evanston, Illinois, in 1958. The C.A.A.C. (College Admissions Assistance Center) was opened in New York in 1959. They are a clearing house for students and colleges **(Jefferson 1962, 23).** Two organizations which give aptitude tests to college bound students have become an integral part of college entrance requirements. A.C.T. (American College Testing Program) and S.A.T. (Scholastic Aptitude Test) give tests that are required by most colleges.

5

A college bound student today should consult one of the many college guide books that are published annually. Lovejoy's College Guide in addition to a capsule description of 3,600 colleges gives career, financial, and special program advice. The College Handbook 1982-83 describes over 3000 colleges giving such information as cost, facilities, and requirements. The complexity of college admission and financing is itself a way of screening students. "Today most college applicants apply concurrently to at least six institutions or more" **(Lovejoy 1981, 9).** Equally important to most students is financial aid; and it is suggested that students make a variety of applications for scholarships, work programs, federal aid, loans, and grants. "At least four and perhaps five sources of income beyond the help from his family may be used by a student to pay college costs. These are scholarships, term-time jobs, summer employment, loans, and spread-out savings" **(Lovejoy 1982, 3).**

BIBLIOGRAPHY

Bell, Laird. 1962. "Admit and Flunk." Atlantic Monthly 210: 54-65.

Chase, W.J. and C.H. Thurber. 1896. "Preliminary Report of the Committee College Entrance Requirements." School Review 4:341-412.

College Entrance Examination Board. 1982. The College Handbook 1982-83. 20th ed. New York: College Entrance Examination Board.

Eliot, Charles. 1890. "The Gap Between the Elementary Schools and the Colleges." N.E.A. Proceedings 29:522-533.

Fischer, H.A. 1890. "Uniform Requirements for Admission." N.E.A. Proceedings 29:705-707.

Fuess, Claude. 1950. The College Board: Its First Fifty Years. New York: Columbia University Press.

Jefferson, J. 1962. "Getting into College." N.E.A. Journal 51:23.

Lovejoy, Clarence. 1981. Lovejoy's College Guide. 15th ed. New York: Simon and Schuster.

----- 1982. Lovejoy's Career and Vocational School Guide. New York: Simon and Schuster.

Moore, F.W. 1902. "The Equalization of the Requirement for Admission into the Different Courses Leading to the First Collegiate Degree." School Review 10:217-223.

N.E.A. 1897. "Round Table on College Entrance Requirements." N.E.A. Proceedings 36:309-316.

Nock, S.A. 1946. "Admission of Non-High School Graduates." Journal of the American Association of Collegiate Registrars 21:390-391.

Traxler, A. and A. Townsend, eds. 1953. Improving Transition from School to College. New York: Harper and Brothers.

NOTES

NOTES

INDEX

(Section numbers in parentheses) *Page*
abbreviations (38)........................17
author-date bibliography (48)..............37
author-date research paper (50)............39
author-date system of notation (43).........35
bibliographic entry, book (34)..............15
bibliographic entry, encyclopedia (36)......16
bibliographic entry, magazine (35)..........16
bibliographic entry, newspaper (37).........16
bibliography (28)..........................13
bibliography, author-date (48)..............37
bibliography, form of (33)..................14
bibliography, kinds of (29).................13
bibliography, sample (33) (45)...........14, 36
book bibliographic entry (34)...............15
book, footnote for (22).....................10
complete bibliography (32)..................14
crediting (17)...............................8
crediting by footnote (19)...................9
crediting in context (18)....................8
encyclopedia article, footnote for (25)......12
encyclopedia bibliographic entry (36).......16
endnote page (41)...........................26
endnote research paper (40).................26
footnote for a book (22)....................10
footnote for a magazine article (23).........11
footnote for an encyclopedia article (25)....12
footnote for a newspaper article (24)........11
footnote, initial reference (26).............12
footnote numbers (21)........................10
footnote, position of (20)....................9
footnote, second and later references (27)..12
ibid. (38)..................................17
identification of paper (8)....................3
initial reference footnote (26)...............12
library paper (1)..............................1

INDEX — (Continued)

magazine article, footnote for (23). 11
magazine bibliographic entry (35). 16
newspaper article, footnote for (24). 11
newspaper bibliographic entry (37). 16
notetaking (5). 2
op. cit. (38). 17
outline, definition of an (11). 4
outline, form of an (13). 5
outline, kinds of (14). 7
outline, purpose of an (12). 4
pagination (7). 3
practical bibliography (30). 14
research paper defined (1). 1
research paper, parts of (3). 2
research paper, procedure for (4). 2
research paper, purpose of (2). 1
sample bibliography (33) (45). 14, 36
sample author-date research paper (50). 39
sample endnote research paper (42). 27
sample footnote research paper (39). 18
second and later reference footnotes (27). . . 12
sentence outline (15). 7
term paper (1). 1
title, placement of (10). 4
title page (9). 4
title page, sample of. 18
topic outline (16). 8
typing (6). 3
working bibliograpy (31). 14